PEOPLE HAVE CHANGED OUR WORLD

MERLE FISCHLOWITZ, PHD

authorHOUSE®

AuthorHouse™
1663 Liberty Drive
Bloomington, IN 47403
www.authorhouse.com
Phone: 833-262-8899

Published by AuthorHouse 02/08/2023

ISBN: 979-8-8230-0029-1 (sc)
ISBN: 979-8-8230-0030-7 (e)

Library of Congress Control Number: 2023901851

Print information available on the last page.

This book is printed on acid-free paper.

DEDICATED TO

MY YOUNGEST GRANDCHILDREN AND
GREAT-GRANCHILDREN,
SUMMER, HANNAH, DELILAH, JUDE,
MIKA, KAINOA, EDEN AND FELIX,
AND THEIR PARENTS.

CONTENTS

INTRODUCTION

The idea to write these essays came as I was completing the Second Edition of <u>Oh, The Changes I Have Seen; My 87 Years of Memories.</u> That memoir of the technology changes I had seen and used in my life led me to realize there were several social and political changes I had also observed.

These essays are not written in an academic style, with citations for all outside sources. Rather, this is a personal memoir, using statistics I've been able to find by use of current internet research. Many of the data used were from various publications by the U.S. Census Bureau, or from comments by public figures.

As I was born in the early years of the Great Depression, I recall seeing men begging on the streets, Work Progress Administration men improving public streets near my elementary school, and Civilian Conservation Corps men working in MO state parks my family visited on vacation. I was aware of the changes around me that showed men going from begging to working.

I don't intend these essays as praise of FDR's New Deal, nor complaint about either political party's policies. I only want to report on social and political changes I've seen as technologies have changed the way we visit with family and friends, communicate with each other, and learn the news.

Merle Fischlowitz

Honolulu, Hawaii, 2023

ACKNOWLEDGEMENTS

I acknowledge the care and teaching from my parents, who never stifled my curiosity about the world around me. I am grateful to all my teachers, some in school and several older friends, who taught me to read, improve my writing, and carefully be aware of details in various places I lived, worked, and sought cultural enrichment. It is my hope that, in some small ways, these essays and my earlier report on changing technologies will guide coming generations to be carefully aware of the changes in their lives and in their communities.

I also acknowledge, with pride, the illustrations on the cover of this book, created in part by my young grandchildren: Hannah Davis, 10; Delilah Davis, 8; and James Kainoa Davis, 6, who helped me choose the copyrighted Apple emoji.

1. WOMEN CHANGED OUR TIMES

"Leave it to Beaver" was a popular family-oriented television show from 1957–1963. The program showed the mother was always at home, shopping, or intervening for her son at school. The father worked an unknown job, but was at home evenings and weekends. This was a typical American family in mid-20th century. During the years I watched that show with my young children most adult American white women stayed home, or worked retail or clerical jobs.

WOMEN IN AMERICAN POLITICS

In 1960 there were 2 women Senators, and 17 Congresswomen, with nearly equal numbers of Republicans and Democrats. Sixty-three years later, as I'm writing this, there are 24 women Senators, and 123 Congresswomen. Senate Democrats out-number Republican women two to one. In the House of Representatives Democrats out-number Republican women three to one.

In 2007, after having served as Congresswoman for 20 years, Nancy Pelosi was elected Speaker of the House of Representatives, a post she held with an 8-year hiatus, 2010-2018, until her retirement from that position in 2022.

After the 2022 election there are now a record number of women in Congress. There will be 124 Congresswomen, including Mrs. Pelosi, in the House of

Representatives, and 25 women Senators. Among the Congresswomen half identify as African-American, Asian-American, Latina, Middle Eastern, or Native American. The following States have no women representing them in Congress: AR, ID, KY, MD, MT, ND, RI, SD, and UT. Arkansas will have its first woman Governor, Sarah H. Sanders, daughter of a former Governor. Republican Kristi Noem was re-elected SD Governor.

Rhode Island's former Governor, Gina Raimondo, Harvard graduate, Rhodes Scholar, graduate of Yale Law School, and venture capitalist, is now Secretary of Commerce in President Biden's Cabinet.

Before 1970 only 4 women were elected Governors of their states, all surrogates for their husbands who had either died or were not eligible for re-election. In 1974 Ella Grasso of Connecticut became the first woman to be elected Governor on her own merits in any state. In 2022 there were 5 Democrat and 3 Republican elected women Governors. After the 2022 elections there will be 12 women state Governors. Arizona, Arkansas, Massachusetts, and New York will each have elected their first female executives.

The United States Supreme Court had no woman Justice until President Reagan named Sandra Day O'Connor in 1980. Since Justice O'Connor first joined the Court 6 women have been or are currently sitting as Justices. O'Connor and Ruth Bader Ginsburg are deceased. There are now 4 women Justices: Amy Coney Barrett, Katanji Brown Jackson, Elena Kagan, and Sonia Sotomayor.

On a local basis, in San Diego County, CA, the key law enforcement officers are both women; Summer Stephan, District Attorney, and newly elected Kelly Martinez, Sherriff, each sworn into office in January, 2023.

AMERICAN WOMEN IN LAW AND MEDICINE

The numbers of women entering legal and medical professions have steadily increased in the past half-century. Only 3% of lawyers were women in 1971. New reports estimate 38% of lawyers are women. Females are about 55% of current law students. Female enrollment data for 1971 are not available.

In 1980 about 12% of physicians were women, but women were already 25% of medical school students. In 2020 reports showed that about 37% of physicians were women, and medical schools had 48% female graduates.

WOMEN IN THE AMERICAN LABOR FORCE

In the half-century since 1970 the percentage of women in the labor force with college degrees quadrupled, while the percentage of male college graduates only doubled. Women's average earnings have always been less than men's. Four decades ago women earned about 62% of men's earnings. Currently women's average earnings are now about 82% of men's earnings. Of course, much of that increase is owed to the increased number of highly educated women in the labor force. As one indicator of change in women's employment, the percentage of women in all STEM (Science, Technology, Engineering and Math) jobs went from 7% in 1970 to 26% in 2020.

But changes have come not only among jobs requiring a college degree. Female employment in law enforcement and (non-professional) medical services has grown substantially in the past half-century. In the construction industry, where there has been a marked increase in the numbers of women employed, the roles they've taken have also changed. Construction occupations are classed as Managerial, Clerical and Support, and Production. This chart shows the changes of women's roles in the construction industry in two decades

% Women in	1985	2005
MANAGERIAL	16%	27%
CLERICAL SUPORT	68%	52%
PRODUCTION	16%	21%

In one particular blue-collar industry, tree-trimming and landscape maintenance, I recently noticed that the company hired for that work at the condominiums where I live was managed by women, including some who worked high in the air on 'cherry pickers' trimming the coconut trees.

3

Recent data have shown that men completed fewer years of formal education than have women. As more women have entered professional jobs in law, medicine, and computer science, men in similar fields have reported more stress in their work. These apparent social changes have been reported in a publication by British author Robert Reeves, in <u>Of Boys and Men,</u> published in 2022 by the Brookings Institution. In this book Reeves sees a need for a new view of masculinity that is compatible with gender equality. This essay author believes such a changed view of masculinity will take a generation of changing education and changing social norms to become reality.

WOMEN AS NATIONAL LEADERS

In the past half-century there has been a large increase in the number of women who have become Heads of State or Heads of Government. There have been 121 women heads of government and/or heads of state in 98 nations since 1949. Of those 121 women leaders only 24 of them served in the 20th century, and 97 have served or are serving in the 22 years of the current century. Of nine regions of the world, Africa, E. Asia, E. Europe, Latin America, Mediterranean, Middle East, N. America, Oceana, S. Asia, Scandinavia, and W. Europe, nations that had been colonized in prior centuries, primarily in South Asia, had the highest rate of women leaders, 38.5%, in the 20th century.

Eastern Europe, including former USSR nations of Estonia, Latvia, Lithuania, and Moldova, plus former communist nations such Croatia, Poland, Romania, and Serbia, also have had 24 women national leaders, 22 of them in this century. Though West European nations have had nearly 16% of all female national leaders, English speaking countries, other than in the Caribbean, have had less than 7% of all women leading nations in the past 70 years.

WOMEN NOBEL LAUREATES

The first woman to be awarded a Nobel Prize was Marie Curie in 1903 who received the award for Physics along with her husband Pierre Curie. The second woman to be awarded a Nobel Prize was Baroness Bertha von Suttner, an Austrian who had written extensively against war in the late 19th century, and was awarded the Nobel Peace Prize in 1905. In 1935 Marie Curie and her daughter Irene Joliot-Curie were awarded the Nobel Prize in Chemistry. In the 90 years since, six other women have received the Nobel Prize in Chemistry, including Emmanuelle Charpentier and Jenifer Doudna in 2020 for their work developing methods of editing genes. When Ms Doudna told her Hilo, Hawaii counselor, in the 1990s, she wanted to study science, the counselor tried to discourage her saying "girls don't do science."

Other women have been awarded Nobel Prizes, including 12 for Physiology or Medicine; 17 in Literature; 17 in Peace; and 2 in Economic Science. Of the 60 women who have been awarded Nobel Prizes in 121 years, 31 of those awards, over 50%, have been made since January, 2000.

WOMEN'S RELATIONS WITH MEN: PRIVATE OR PUBLIC?

In the author's 90 years of life in a society of women and men it has been his experience that certain individualized relations between one man and one woman are kept private. These have included deciding when casual dating might become a commitment to marriage; choosing when to have children; and sharing information about pregnancy; and childbirth. It is my observation since growth of 'social media,' and the ubiquitous cell phone as camera, that the line between private and public decisions and actions has become far less distinct.

As examples I offer the following now common public, or semi-public events. From my beachfront balcony I've recently seen a highly staged marriage proposal, with multiple friends taking photos of the blindfolded 'surprised' woman being led to a party where her male friend has posted a large sign reading "Marry Me!"

Destination weddings, where the wedding party travel to a special resort, with staging of what once was a religious ceremony viewed by families and friends, have become more frequent among upper middle-class couples. A photographic record to be shared on social media is one key purpose of the event.

When a woman is pregnant and feels secure enough in that pregnancy and, thanks to modern medicine, may know the sex of her baby, that news had been shared in private with immediate family, grandparents to be, and the couple's siblings. Now there are 'Gender Reveal' parties, with balloons, festivities, and of course many photographs to mark the event for several friends, acquaintances, and co-workers, all shared on social media.

When I first became a father in 1956 and 1958 childbirth was witnessed only by doctors and nurses. When I again became a father in 1975 I was present at my daughter's birth, after having been with my wife in natural childbirth classes. I wonder if childbirth may become a semi-public event, with photos to be shared on social media.

This male author recalls a time when women determined the nature and social awareness of a relationship with a loved one, whether male or female. With social media and instant video access to family and friends world-wide, young children come to accept as normal the sharing of once private family events with a growing number of viewers. Have these technology advances so blurred the lines between private and public acts that women no longer are able to set such boundaries?

2. DEMOGRAPHICS

In the 1997 publication <u>Guns, Germs, and Steel,</u> author Jared Diamond wrote a comprehensive history of world societies that showed how availability of fertile land, domesticated animals, natural resources, and regional topography combined to allow certain communities to rise to positions of dominance in various eras of human history. This excellent publication gave rise to the theory of Geographic Determinism.

I offer a variation on Diamond's theory, suggesting that Demographics have played nearly as important a role as geography and natural resources in influencing evolution of modern nations. Demographics is understood to mean statistical data that describe populations and their characteristics. Those characteristics include birthrate, life expectancy, ethnic identity, levels of education, religious affiliation, and other data. I believe Demographics had an influence on the strength of nations since the end of the Middle Ages, possibly as early as the religious conflicts that established Christianity as dominant in Europe and Islam as dominant in what is known as the Middle East.

There is general agreement that Middle Ages refers to the period from 450 of the Common Era, the fall of the Roman Empire, until about mid 16th century. In just 200 years three major events began what we know as the Modern Age.

The fall of Constantinople in 1453, ceding rule by the Greek Eastern Christian church to newly rising Islam was one mark of the end of the Middle Ages.

Invention of the printing press by Johannes Gutenberg, around 1454 is thought to be one starting point for the Modern Age.

The 1648 Treaty of Westphalia that established generally agreed national boundaries in most of Europe in my opinion marks the definite start of modern European society.

One example of demographic influence on society occurred before the end of the middle ages. The Bubonic Plague, or Black Death, spread through nearly all Europe from 1347-1353. Though this pandemic lasted only six years, about one-third of the population of Europe died during that time. It is of interest today that the end of Bubonic Plague was due largely to voluntary quarantine of people in most cities of Europe. That great reduction in population allowed increased food production to bring good nutrition and increase in population to the majority of people who survived.

The end of the Bubonic Plague marked the beginning of what is known as the Renaissance. Improved nutrition for plague survivors, discovery of old Greek texts, and establishment of a unified banking system all combined to make 15th century Florence, Italy, a leading city for trade, arts, and intellectual growth. Once independent parts of the Roman Catholic church got new vitality by strengthening the papal authority in Rome. Populations grew in the various Italian ducal cities. The new printing press allowed the spread of knowledge, including translations of rediscovered Greek works such as Ptolemy's Geography brought to Florence in 1396 by a learned Greek teacher.

The coincidental confluence of birth of Leonardo da Vinci, 1452, Fall of Constantinople, 1453, and invention of the printing press, 1454, started the 'high renaissance' in Italy. Greek mathematics helped artists develop work showing perspective.

Greek geography stimulated wishes to explore new lands, culminating in an age of discovery through the late 16th century. Portuguese began in about 1460 to explore the West coast of Africa. Vasco de Gama of Portugal reached India in 1498, and his voyage showed spices from Asia could be got by sea. Spain commissioned Italian navigator Cristoforo Colombo, who had read translated Greek geography, to sail West in 1492 to seek a new route to India.

These explorations brought Europe gold and slaves from Africa and new fruit and vegetables from the land named for Italian geographer Amerigo Vespucci. Columbus' later voyages brought knowledge of the North American continent. Circumnavigation of the world by Magellan's ships, 1519-1522, confirmed to Europeans the variety of cultures, climates, and peoples in a spherical Earth. The fracturing of the Christian church, a result of the Holy Scriptures being printed in various languages, brought migrations by people of different beliefs for varied reasons from Europe to the Americas.

BIRTHRATE EFFECTS ON NATIONS' SOCIETIES

Ever since society's rulers collected taxes the ruling class wanted to know the population of their realm. Keeping accurate records of population varied by geography, literacy, and other factors. By the early 19th century scholars knew that birthrate, fertility rate, and life expectancy were measures of a society's well-being. Birth rates are shown as number of live births per 1,000 population. Total fertility rate is the number of live births an individual woman has in her lifetime. Life expectancy is the average age of death within a given community.

As records of national populations have become more common, and mortality or age of death more generally known, statisticians have been able to show, and to some extent predict, the impact of changes in these data.

In the United States there has been relatively accurate census data since 1790. There have also been records of immigration to the U.S. since the mid 19th century. Scholars agree that the total fertility rate, TFR, or number of live births each woman has in her life, needs to be 2.1 per woman for a given population in a given area to merely maintain its size from one generation to the next. As urban and rural living conditions have changed, and improved medical services became more commonly available, the birth rate in America varied from an estimated high of 55 per thousand population in 1800 to a recent low of fewer than 14 births per thousand population in 2000. Total Fertility Rate declined as well, with estimates of 5 to 6 births per woman in the mid 19ᵗʰ century to lows of 2.7 to 2.8 births per woman in the 1930s. Census reports of 1950 and 1960 show TFR rose to 2.9 and 3.5 births per woman. However, since 2000 American TFR dropped below 2.1 births per woman, White women having the lowest TFR when data are separated by ethnic identity.

ECONOMIC EFFECTS OF BIRTHRATE CHANGES

As I wrote these essays in late 2022 recent economic data show mixed signals for the near-term health of the American economy. Despite inflation higher than in 40 years, spending by households is still at the usual rates for Christmas holiday season. The unemployment rate, reported 12/1/22 of 3.7%, is at a fifty-year record low, and the number of open jobs is high. Recent census reports show the Covid pandemic was part of the decrease in USA population growth in the three years, 2019-2022. In addition, these census reports show that national population growth in 2022 from immigration of over 870,000 people increase from 2021, accounted for three times as many added people as 'natural growth rate,' or the net number of births over deaths in 2022.

In the words of Brookings Institution demographer William Frey, the United States "would have been back to almost flat-line growth if not for this immigration."

It is the author's opinion that these apparent mixed economic signals, high inflation, low unemployment, and good household spending, are partly the result of reduced birthrate of the past half-century. Despite many mothers stopping work to care for children during the Covid pandemic, the number of two-earner households is still high, and number of children per household is much less than in the 'stagflation' of 1978-1981.

ETHNIC VARIATION IN HIGHER EDUCATION

U.S. Census reports show differences in completion of four-year college education by race and gender. White women and men, and black women, had doubled their rates of college completion in 30 years from 1970–2000. Black men had increased their rate of college completion by only one-fifth. Those changes over 30 years, a full generation, are likely associated with the relationship of declining birthrate with level of education. It should also be noted that Latinos had a greater percentage increase in numbers graduating from college, again more women than men, than did black students. Of all ethnicities, more women than men younger than 65, now have four-year college degrees. By 2020, 36.8% of men had earned such a degree, but 38.3% of all women had earned a four-year degree, illustrating a continued trend of more women than men completing four years of college.

POPULATION DENSITY

The United States is NOT among the 50 most densely populated countries in the world, in terms of people per square mile. However, the USA is the third largest nation in the world in area, smaller than only Russia and Canada. The 50 states are very different in urban and rural areas. The number of people per square mile is called "population density." In our 50 states population density varies from 1,260/ sq mi (NJ) and 1,059/sq mi (RI) down to 5.96/sq mi (WY) and 1.28/sq mi (AK.)

AGRICULTURAL WORKERS

In the past century there has been a dramatic shift in numbers of persons needed to produce agricultural products for human and animal food, and for industrial use. The first year, 1920, the U.S. Census measured farm population, 30% of the U.S. population of about 106 million, lived on farms. In 1950 only

15% population of the 151 million U.S. population lived on farms. These data show that the number of people living on farms went from about 31.8 million in 1920 to fewer than 22.6 million in 1950. Census bureau data show in a later seven-year period, 1970–1977, in the contiguous 48 states, the number of people living on farms dropped by 18.5%, leaving only about 8.5 to 9 million people living on farms. Yet, even with declining American farm population the United States is the largest agricultural exporter in the world.

MEDICAL PROFESSION PAY RELATED TO POPULATION CHANGES

Medical profession earnings changed as response to population growth. There were shortages of nurses and some physicians in hospitals as population grew faster than medical education did. This chart shows estimated average annual earnings for two medical professions in the last 50 to 60 years.

License	Years	1950	1970	1990	2010
RN		$2,300	$5,500	$33,000	$64,000
MD, Family Practice		$12,000	N/A	$96,000	$240,000

While average earnings for RNs increased nearly 300% in sixty years, income for family practice doctors grew only 200% in the same period. These two factors probably cause that disparity. As discussed in a separate essay on how Women Changed our Times, there are about three times as many women physicians in 2020 than there were in 1980. As a result of employment and social changes from the Covid pandemic, hospitals, the largest place of employment for RNs, are competing for far fewer RN professionals in the labor force.

EFFECT OF DEMOGRAPHIC CHANGES ON NATIONAL GROWTH

The established fact that a community or nation needs to have 2.1 births per woman in a given period of time to stay the same size, and current trends show the United States and many industrialized nations have TFR, total fertility rates, below that number, means that those nations will not grow in population, and not increase their labor forces, in the coming generation. As long as nations continue to compete for economic and political leadership those industrialized nations will grow only by absorbing immigrants from other nations and other cultures. If nations do not grow by birth rate or by immigration, each nation's society will become older, with a smaller labor force to create an economy strong enough to support elderly populations. There are examples of nations with increasingly elderly populations. One key metric that indicates a nation's aging population is the percent of population over age 65. Of the 12 most populated nations, all with over 100 million people, four of those countries have more than 10% of people older than 65.

They are China, USA, Russia, and Japan. The other 8 large nations, in order of population size, showing percent of people older than 65 are India, 6.1%; Indonesia, 5.6%; Pakistan, 4.3%; Brazil, 8.5%; Nigeria, 2.7%; Bangladesh, 5.1%; Mexico, 7.2%; and Ethiopia, 3.5%.

All four large aging countries have a current TFR below 2.1 children per woman. Yet all of them have increasing levels of technological capabilities. Of the eight large nations who do not have aging populations note that Brazil, India, and Mexico, each has increasingly high levels of technological capabilities.

Though demographic data do not cause societal changes, analysis of such data makes judgments more reliable. It is this author's opinion that unless the United States opens its borders to more educated immigrants, we will have increased economic competition from nations such as Brazil, India, and Mexico.

MERLE FISCHLOWITZ, PH.D.

EDUCATION AFFECTS NATIONAL DEMOGRAPHIC CHANGES

The best universities in the world have for centuries been in Europe and in the United States. Since the founding of universities at Oxford and Cambridge in Britain and Bologna and Padua in Italy, between 1096 and 1222, there have been centers of learning in created to study non-religious subjects such as Greek and Latin languages, astronomy, geography, history, literature, mathematics, philosophy, and science.

The oldest university in America is Harvard, founded in 1636 by Puritan congregational leaders. The United States encouraged the growth of public education by various legislative acts in the 19th and 20th centuries.

In the late 20th century, after WW2, there was a large influx of international students to American universities. Recent records show large increases of post-graduate degrees granted to international students. In 2018 American university records show large number of students from these countries:

Student numbers	From
Over 200,000	China
100,00-199,000	India
10,000-99,999	Each, from: Brazil, Canada, Japan, Nigeria, Saudi Arabia, South Korea, and Vietnam.

International graduate students in Science and Engineering courses grew from 24.8% in 2000 to 58.7% of those graduate students in 2015. Although these data represent temporary visa holders, in the USA only as long as they are in school, many of them got work in the USA after completion of their education.

These data show two distinct trends. One is that America has become a greatly diversified society in the past 70 years, although the extent of cultural and ethnic diversification varies in different regions of our nation. The other trend this author has noted is that other nations, particularly those that send their youth to study in our universities, are increasingly competitive with the USA.

The author poses this question: Will increased ethnic variations in American society help or hinder our nation to maintain its leadership role in the world in political and economic terms?

3. IMMIGRATION

I first became aware that people came from different nations in the late 1930s, when Jewish relatives arrived in my hometown of St. Louis MO, as refugees from Nazi dominated Germany and Austria. When attending Grinnell College I met students from Afghanistan, Germany, Ghana, Jordan, and Taiwan, most of whom returned to their homelands after graduate degrees, but some of whom stayed in the United States, as physicians, writers, and in other professions. In recent years, in the United States and in parts of the European Union, there has been growing opposition to increases of non-white immigrants and those from different cultures.

There have been different reasons for increased immigration to Europe, the United Kingdom, and the United States. Many of the finest universities in the world are in the United States, United Kingdom, and in other European nations, attracting young men and women from many nations seeking good education. Also, many labor-intensive industries, and industrialized agriculture, are in these nations and need less-educated laborers for production.

The growing extent of immigration from many lands into American and European nations is a result of various political and economic factors. In 1949 ten European nations formed the Council of Europe. In 1957 six of those nations founded the European Common Market. The UK's attempts to join the Common Market in 1963 and 1967 were vetoed by French president de Gaulle. After de Gaulle retired in 1969 the UK's admission to the European Economic Community was ratified in 1972, and approved by popular referendum in 1975.

The European Union included 28 nations after admission of Croatia in 2009.

In 2016 the United Kingdom held a referendum, called Brexit, on whether to leave the European Union. The three major causes of the UK wanting to leave the European Union were a sense of loss of sovereignty; growing immigration from different cultures; and general anti-establishment opinions. The Brexit referendum to leave the EU passed with only 51.8% of the vote. Historical data show that foreign born UK residents rose from less than 6% in 1971 to 12.8% in 2011. Some surveys at the time of Brexit vote showed that immigration was the leading cause of "leave" votes. Recent reports from the UK Office of Budget Responsibility, and from other economic analysts in Britain, show that the UK economy has decreased 9% to 18% since Brexit in 2021. This decrease in UK Gross Domestic Product and in international trade appear to be a direct result of reduced trade with the European Union

In the recent upheavals of United Kingdom governments, from Prime Ministers Boris Johnson (2019-2022), Liz Truss (August-October, 2022) to Rishi Sunak's 2022 election, there was an increase of cabinet members who had not been born in the UK. In PM Johnson's first cabinet there was one non-UK born member, and five who were first born of immigrant parents. In the seven-week tenure of Liz Truss as Prime Minister there were two cabinet members not born in the UK, plus five more who were children of immigrants. After PM Truss' resignation in October her successor Rishi Sunak is a UK born son of Punjabi Indian immigrants from Africa. In his cabinet he has so far retained one non-UK born member and 3 UK born children of UK immigrants as members in his cabinet. Sunak is the first non-white Prime Minister in British history.

At a recent royal palace event a 'lady in waiting' to the late Queen Elizabeth 2 was heard to insult a Black U.K. born woman, founder of a charity supporting women, by asking "Where are you really from?" As result of that widely reported incident the elderly white woman resigned from her palace duties.

Latest census data from England and Wales show that less than 50% of the population in those two parts of U.K. identify themselves as Christian. In 2021 only 46% of the population did so, compared with 53% in 2011. The largest change was of those identifying themselves as having 'no religion,' going from 25% in 2011 to 37% in 2021. In the 2021 report Muslims represent 6.5%; Hindus 1.6%; and Sikhs and Jews each fewer than one percent of English and Welsh population.

The UK and the USA had large changes of immigrant populations in the past 50 years. UK foreign-born population rose from 5.8%, 1970, to 16.8%, 2020. USA foreign born population rose from 4.7%, 1970, to 13.7%, 2020.

MIGRATION WITHIN THE EUROPEAN UNION

The Schengen Agreement of 1985 including Belgium, France, Germany, Luxembourg and The Netherlands, authorized gradual abolition of visa reviews at their common borders. Additions to the Agreement came into effect September 1, 1993, and were incorporated into European Community law May 1, 1999. Since the original Schengen Agreement all EU nations plus non-EU nations Iceland, Liechtenstein, Norway and Switzerland have signed the Schengen Agreement.

Since the full implementation of that visa-free agreement for citizens of the signatory nations several EU nations that were original signers, such as France, Germany, Hungary, and Slovakia, have had anti-immigrant protests.

Conservative anti-immigrant governments have been elected in Bosnia and Herzegovina, Croatia, Hungary, and Serbia.

IMMIGRANTS IN USA BUSINESSES

Immigrants in the U.S. achieved noteworthy accomplishments in business, education, and science. In 2022 among the Fortune 500 companies 102 were founded by immigrants, and another 117 were founded by children of immigrants. Some businesses founded by immigrants are

- Anheuser–Busch, 1879, by German immigrants Eberhard Anheuser and Adolphus Busch;
- AT&T (Bell Telephone) 1875, by Scottish immigrant Alexander G. Bell;
- Big Lots, 1967, by Russian immigrant Sol Shenk;
- Capital One, 1994, by British immigrant Nigel Morris;
- Colgate, 1873, by British immigrant William Colgate;
- EBAY, 1995, by French immigrant Pierre Omidyar;
- Google, 1998, by Russian immigrant Sergei Brin;
- Kohls, 1962, by Polish immigrant Maxwell Kohl;
- Kraft Foods, 1923, by Canadian immigrant James Kraft;
- Panda Express, 1985, by Chinese immigrants Andrew and Peggy Cheng;
- Pfizer, 1849, by German immigrant Charles Pfizer;
- Tesla, 2002, by South African immigrant Elon Musk;
- YAHOO, 1994, by Taiwanese immigrant Jerry Yang.

In 2020 BoardroomInsiders.com reported 45% of Fortune 500 companies' Chief Executives are immigrants or children of immigrants. This sample shows some of these companies, CEOs, and CEO national origin.

CORP	CEO	NATIONAL ORIGIN
Abbot Laboratories	Robert Ford	Brazil
Biogen Inc.	Michel Vounatsos	Morocco
Bristol-Myers Squibb	Giovanni Caforio	Italy
Broadcom Inc.	Hock Tan	Malaysia
Clorox	Benno Dorer	Germany
Estee Lauder Inc.	Fabrizio Freda	Italy

Flour Corp.	Carlos Hernandez	Cuba
Google	Sundar Pichal	India
Honeywell, Inc.	Darius Adamcyk	Poland
HP, Inc.	Enrique Loves	Spain
IBM Corp.	Arvind Krishna	India
Kraft Heinz Co.	Miquel Patricio	Portugal
Microsoft Corp.	Satya Nadella	India
NVIIDIA Corp.	Jen-Hsun Huang	Taiwan
Oracle Corp	Safra Catz	Israel
PepsiCo Inc.	Ramon Lauarta	Spain
SAIC	Nazzic Keene	Libya
Uber Tech. Inc.	Dara Khosrowshahi	Iran
Verizon Inc.	Hans Vestberg	Sweden
Walgreen-Boots, Inc.	Stafano Pessina	Italy

IMMIGRANTS IN USA EDUCATION AND SCIENCE

The Association of American Universities, representing major research institutions, in 2011 reported 11of their 61 member universities had foreign born presidents. Since then two other leading schools, Rice University, and University of CA, San Diego, named foreign born leaders.

In the 121 years that Nobel Prizes have been awarded, many immigrants in America have been Nobel Laureates. Of all Nobel Prizes awarded in Chemistry, Medicine, and Physics since 2000, American immigrants were 37% Nobel laureates in those fields.

IMMIGRANTS IN USA POLITICS

Though no foreign-born person may be President one candidate, John McCain, was born to U.S. citizens at a US Navy base in the Panama Canal Zone, and was thus a Natural Born Citizen. One recent President, Barack Obama, was born in Hawai'i to an immigrant father from Kenya and an American citizen mother. The current Vice-President, Kamala Harris, first woman to hold that office, is the American born child of immigrant parents. One recent First Lady, Melania Trump, was an immigrant from Slovenia.

Being an American natural born citizen is not a requirement for any other elected or appointed office in the United States. In 2022 the President's Cabinet includes Marty Walsh, Secretary of Labor, son of Irish immigrants; Miguel Cardona, Secretary of Education, born in Connecticut to parents from Puerto Rico; Alejandro Mayorkas, Secretary of Homeland Security, born in Cuba; Katherine Tai, U.S, Trade Representative, born in Connecticut to parents from Taiwan; and Arati Prabakar, Director of Science and Technology Policy, born in India.

Other immigrants served in presidential cabinets. Alexander Hamilton, Treasury Secretary, born in West Indies, and James McHenry, of Ireland, Secretary of War, were both in George Washington's administration. Albert Gallitin, Swiss born, was Secretary of the Treasury in the Jefferson administration. Other foreign-born cabinet officials were German born Henry Kissinger, and Czech born Madeline Albright, each Secretary of State.

As various nations have economic stress and/or significant changes in ethnic or religious population groups those nations often enact restrictive immigration laws.

This author asks when will people in our nation recognize that all of us, except descendants of Native Americans, Inuit in Alaska, and Polynesians in Hawaii, are children of immigrants, or even recent immigrants citizens?

4. INTEGRATE OR DISINTEGRATE

When I was in high school in the 1940s there were a few 'integrated" schools around town. The school I attended and a few neighboring schools had Catholic, Jewish, and Protestant students. There were not any black schools in St. Louis County, but there were two all black high schools and several black elementary schools in the City of St. Louis. Much of St. Louis County had restrictive covenants setting some neighborhoods as not welcoming Jews. The Supreme Court declared restrictive covenants unconstitutional in 1948, but most realtors tried to keep neighborhoods clear of unwanted buyers.

Seventy-four years after I graduated high school there is now one newly elected African-American Governor (MD) and there have been three African-American Governors, (MA, NY and VA) since 1990. New MD Governor Wes Moore is joined by Lt. Gov. Aruna Miller, who as young girl immigrated from India. Among other non-white Governors there have been, since 1990, four Asian-Americans (in HI, LA, SC, and WA); four Mexican-Americans (2 each in NM and NV); and one Native American, in OK. Since 1948 there have been nine African-American Senators, three presently serving from GA, NJ, and SC. One former African-American Senator became President. There have been three African-American Supreme Court Justices, two of whom are currently serving.

In the 1960s a physician I knew in St. Louis went across the river to Illinois to stand witness for the marriage of two colleagues, a Chinese-American man and his white bride. There was a law in Missouri, and in several other states, against miscegenation, or inter-racial marriage.

Only in 1967 did the U.S. Supreme Court declared laws against inter-racial marriage unconstitutional, under protections assured by the 14th Amendment to the U.S. Constitution. Interestingly, since 1991 an African-American man who is married to a white woman has been a Supreme Court Justice.

As I wrote this, African-American Congresswoman Karen Bass was elected the first woman to become mayor of Los Angeles, the second largest city in our still integrating nation. When she took office the four largest cities in our nation, New York City, Los Angeles, Chicago, and Houston, all have African-American mayors, two of them women. Other visible signs, but not obvious to all viewers, as indicators of our changing culture have been the increase of Black and Latino characters in comic strips and advertising; open media discussion about the roles and presentations for Asian, Black, and Latino actors; and a gradual, if regional, lessening of a politician's or community leader's race being noted as important in media.

AFRICAN-AMERICAN INSTITUTIONS AS PART OF AMERICAN CULTURE

In recent years, even before Howard University alumna Kamala Harris became our first woman, and first African-American Vice President, there has been recognition of historically Black Colleges and Universities, referred to as HBCUs. In late 2022 a kerfuffle was created by the resignation of a highly successful African-American football coach from one HBCU to take a similar position at a predominately White university. Many Blacks saw that move as disloyalty to HBCUs. Yet, there have been other sports media that focus on the low numbers of African-American coaches in professional sports where a large number of players are Black. The author wonders if Black activists in America want further integration of African-American sports leaders, or the strengthening and preservation of HBCUs as separate, largely segregated schools.

CONSERVATIVE BACKLASH MOVEMENTS

Since 2015 there have been movements alleging laws for affirmative action and against racial discrimination are against white people and traditional American culture. Some events during the Trump presidency, 2017-2021, were evidence of anti-Black, anti-Muslim, and anti-Semitic cultural attitudes and occasional organized group actions. Since the beginning of the Biden administration some new laws, enacted as financial remedies for losses during the Covid pandemic, attempted to prioritize benefits for 'socially disadvantaged' groups, intended to mean people of color, Blacks or Latinos. In 2022 there have been legal actions, some successful, to nullify the discrimination in such laws. Some of the laws have been re-written to apply equally to all workers or businesses economically harmed by the pandemic.

MELTING POT OR BOUILLAISSE?

When I was a young student the idea was very common, and generally accepted, that America would become a 'melting pot,' where many cultures would blend and become alike. Since the 1960s, largely due to the "Black Pride" movement, there has been increasing awareness of the unique qualities of the many different cultures flourishing in our nation. In my hometown of St. Louis there were a few Chinese restaurants, where 'chop suey,' and other somewhat oriental dishes were served. The serving staff were mostly Caucasian, while the cooks were Asian.

The only other 'ethnic' restaurants in St. Louis were Italian, and most were in a neighborhood, known as 'The Hill,' where many Italian immigrants had settled in the late 19th century. Visiting St. Louis in the 1980s I found more Chinese, and Japanese, restaurants, and was surprised when friends suggested we go to a new Korean restaurant.

In many ways our culture has changed from a 'melting pot' where all blend together to be more alike, to become a 'bouillabaisse,' a French seafood mixture of ingredients where each retains its own flavor. In major urban areas there are now choices and varieties of restaurants, local festivals, and holiday celebrations among African-American, Chinese, Japanese, Latin American, Mexican, and many European cultures.

What way will our nation's culture go? Will future generations of Americans acknowledge and accept diverse cultures from a variety of immigrants, or will there be a social-political divide expressing opposition to an increasingly diverse culture in an interconnected world? I have explored some of these contrasting movements in the last essay in this book: "Our Somewhat United States."

5. OUR SOMEWHAT UNITED STATES

Following is an expanded letter I wrote to a European friend who asked me in early 2022 to explain and clarify for him the mixed political-social climate of the United States, as seen from Europe.

EARLY HISTORY

To reply to your concerns about the fractured nature of American politics today I think it important you learn and understand about the various peoples who came here, their reasons for coming, their various cultural and national origins, and the nature of community organizations they developed.

The first European settlers along the Atlantic coast were two distinctly different groups of people. The earliest permanent settlement was at Jamestown, Virginia, in 1607, named for King James 1 of the United Kingdom. King James had approved the formation of a stockholders group, "The London Company," to settle new lands in North America. The Jamestown settlers built a fort to protect themselves from presumed hostile savages. They formed a governing council of men, who King James named in their charter. By 1638 these settlers had established Williamsburg, a city that became the capitol city of the Virginia colony until 1780.

Another group of early settlers are known as the Puritans. This group started in England in late 16th century, objecting to rituals of the Church of England. They wanted to return to a 'pure form of Christianity,' with no special status for ministers and a stricter morality than seen among Church of England members.

In 1607, the same year Jamestown was founded, a small group of Puritans left England for Leiden in Holland.

There they found work in the clothing industry, but also felt the time required for work prevented their having enough time for religious observance. In 1621 the Puritans in Holland rented a cargo ship, the Mayflower, from the Plymouth Co, a part of the London Company who had financed the Virginia settlers. They sailed from Holland to what became known as New England, 600 miles North of Jamestown. The ship rental agreement required the Puritans to send fish and furs back to England as payment for rental of the Mayflower. The Puritan settlers named the settlement Massachusetts Bay Colony, adapting the native Algonquin term for the area. Other Puritans followed in the 1630s as King Charles I turned the Church of England to more Catholic-like rituals. More immigration from England also came for more economic opportunities, not found in the United Kingdom in the current religious turmoil.

In 1619 the San Juan Bautista, a Spanish ship captured by the British navy, landed at what is now Hampton, VA. The ship had about two dozen Africans who had been captured in West Africa and were traded as commodities to English settlers in exchange for ship's supplies. Though a few Africans settled in Virginia as 'indentured servants' (meaning a contract was 'signed' by the worker showing his bite, or denture.) most Africans were treated as slaves and worked on English owned lands. As the Virginia colony grew, the agricultural produce was largely the result of slave labor.

One example of northern industry as different from southern agriculture was that in the mid 18th century Paul Revere, a silversmith in Boston, developed mass production techniques for making rifles and pistols. Those and other manufactured items were traded to southern colonies for agricultural produce.

After a century of colonization the northern colonies were not as strictly puritan in their religious observance as they had been when first settled, yet the congregational manner of religious organization extended to local politics and social organizations. In the southern colonies, founded by proprietors who owed allegiance to the King of England, who had proprietorial authority over colonists, that social nature of cooperative governance did not develop.

EARLY 19TH CENTURY DEVELOPMENT

Southern states in the newly independent country depended on agriculture both to feed and clothe themselves, but also as a primary export to England. Cotton for the new clothing industry in the United Kingdom was a major export of the Southern states. Cotton was grown, bundled and brought to ports mostly by slave labor, using horse-drawn vehicles for land transport. In Northern states where land and seasons were not as friendly to major agricultural development, small manufacturing and trade became the main basis of economic growth.

The desire to collect fur and timber from Western regions spurred development of canals. The Erie Canal, from Albany NY on the Hudson River to Buffalo NY on Lake Erie was promoted in the NY state legislature by DeWitt Clinton. Funds were appropriated and work on the canal began in 1817. When the 363-mile canal was finished in 1825 then Governor Clinton carried a barrel of Lake Erie water on a canal boat to New York City where he emptied it into the Atlantic Ocean, calling this "the marriage of the waters."

Shortly after the Erie Canal was completed the first steam railroads were built in America. The first train company was the Baltimore and Ohio, built to explore new territories in Kentucky and Ohio, and bring produce from those areas to Eastern seaports for export, and trade among more populated states. Railroad construction was a major industry from 1840 – 1860.

When the War Between the States began in 1861, states in the North had over 22,000 miles of railroad track. States in the Confederacy had slightly over

9,500 miles of track. That difference in railroad development was one major reason the North prevailed in that war.

EARLY 19TH CENTURY IMMIGRATION

Nearly all the colonial settlers from England were Protestants, members of the Church of England, or the puritan Congregational Church. The first Lord Baltimore, George Calvert, (1580-1632) was a secret Catholic, and had estates in Ireland and in England. He maintained favor with King James I by his work in international relations with France, Holland, and Spain. George Calvert had at first tried to colonize part of what is now Newfoundland, Canada, but the cold climate made his work fruitless. He then asked for a Royal Charter for the part of Virginia around Chesapeake Bay, but the Virginia settlers strongly opposed that. As a result he was given a Royal Charter to settle the area between the populated Virginia colony and Southern Pennsylvania. The new Maryland colony had open toleration for other religious beliefs. Tradition shows that both Anglicans and Catholics were among the first settlers. In 1649 the first Act of Toleration in any colony was passed by Maryland legislature, forbidding actions against "any Christian believing in the divinity of Jesus and the Holy Trinity."

Although this specifically did not apply to Unitarians, a newly formed church, or Jews, attitudes creating the Act of Toleration persisted in Maryland, even during the Cromwell period, 1649-1660, in England.

After the Revolutionary War, the newly created United States of America needed to create a national government, to unite the thirteen separate once British colonies. In 1787 a convention met in Philadelphia which, after many months of discussion, the delegates created the United States Constitution. The First Amendment, among the ten known as the Bill of Rights, ratified in 1791, stated "Congress shall pass no law respecting establishment of religion or prohibiting the free exercise thereof." Much of the support for this statement was based on the 1649 Maryland Act of Toleration.

Most immigration to the United States in early 19th century was from the British Isles. In the 1840s two separate events in Europe affected the nature of the immigration to the U.S.

In 1845 mold disease attacked the potato crops of Ireland, part of the United Kingdom. Although governed as part of the U.K. mostly Catholic Ireland was allowed to send only Anglicans to represent them in London. New laws tried to lower the costs to import food to Ireland, but as result of crop failure and increased cost of imported food about one million people died of starvation or disease by 1850. Those who could left the island to come to the United States to make new lives for themselves.

In central Europe many newly prosperous business people resented the autocratic rulers and the ways taxes were collected. Several protests tried to change rulers' policies, but protestors were overcome by royalist forces.

In these Roman Catholic Southern German communities many of those central European business people sought new freedoms in the United States.

Thus the Irish Potato Famine and the 1848 European revolutions caused many Catholics to come to the U.S. Laborers from Ireland stayed largely in the Northeastern states, where there was need for workers in new factories. Many of the German Catholic business people looked for opportunities in the newly opened Western regions of the U.S., from Ohio to Iowa, Wisconsin, and Missouri. Cities on the Great Lakes; Detroit, Cleveland, and Milwaukee; as well as St. Louis on the Mississippi River, had abundant fresh water, and open routes for shipping by water to the Atlantic Ocean and the Gulf of Mexico.

Among the early settlers in the Western states were German families, named Anheuser, Blatz, Busch, Miller, Pabst and Schlitz. Among the Irish who settled in the Boston, New York and Baltimore areas were families named Biden, Buchanan, Byrnes, Cahill, Carter, Clinton, Curry, Dunne, Kennedy, Leahy, McCarthy, Moynihan, and Reagan. Not all those families were politically active in the 19th century but they all can trace their roots to immigration before 1860.

POLITICAL PARTIES

Before 1850 politicians representing the mostly rural Southern newly independent states aligned themselves with the Democrat-Republican party, that had been started by Presidents Jefferson, Madison, and Monroe. By the 1840s they were named the Democrat party. The Federalist party, of John Adams, had disappeared during the first two decades of the 19th century.

Northern business interests formed the Whig Party, that first elected President Wm. H. Harrison in 1840.

The Whigs also elected Zachary Taylor in 1848, but both of Harrison and Taylor died in office and were succeeded by Vice Presidents John Tyler in 1841 and Millard Fillmore in 1850. The increasing division in the nation on slavery and its political consequences tore the Whigs into two conflicting parts. In the 1850s, as the slavery issue was ripping American political parties apart, there arose another group known as the Order of the Star Spangled Banner, called the American Party. It was a secret society whose members were determined to return the U.S. to a completely Protestant society. If any man were asked if he belonged to such a group he said "I know nothing" so this group was called the "No Nothing Party." Although short-lived, their xenophobic anti-Catholic beliefs and actions were the first sign of a strictly nativist American political force.

In 1854 a group of Northern Whigs and other anti-slavery leaders met in Ripon, WI, and formed the new Republican party, to oppose slavery. Their first presidential candidate in 1856, John Fremont, lost to Democrat James Buchanan, in a three-way contest including the American Party. The second Republican presidential candidate, Abraham Lincoln, won the 1860 election.

The War Between the States, 1861-1865, kept the USA as a politically unified country. Lincoln's Emancipation Proclamation of 1863, and the 13th, 14th, and 15th Amendments to the Constitution outlawed slavery, and technically declared all people born in the United States as equal under the law. Yet nativist, anti-Catholic and anti-Negro attitudes still prevailed in the Southern states and in some areas of Northern States. The increased industrialization of the late 19th and early 20th centuries changed communities in Northern states much more than in Southern states. A major political change also occurred during the late 19th and early 20th centuries.

The Republican party became the dominant political group in the industrialized, more urban Northern states. The newly revived Democrat party was still centered in the once slave-holding states.

In the 64 years from 1868 to 1932 all Presidents except two were Republicans, pro-business, for protective tariffs, and financial stability. Only two men, Grover Cleveland in 1884 and 1892, and Woodrow Wilson in 1912 and 1916 were Democrats elected President, as results of greatly different reasons.

America's involvement in the first World War slowly brought a new awareness of the USA's influence in a wider world. In the 1920s different economic events in Germany, the United Kingdom, and the United States set the stage for world-wide depression starting in 1930. As a result of the perceived Republican responsibility for the stock market crash of 1929 that led to the Great Depression, Franklin Roosevelt and the Democrat party were brought to power in 1933, both in Congress and the White House. Roosevelt's Democrat party was an alliance of Southern pro-segregation legislators and Northern pro-labor politicians. Each group favored federal support for farmers in their own regions. As FDR's 'New Deal' guided America out of the depression, Southern states began to get industrialization from the Tennessee Valley Authority and the Rural Electrification Administration that brought electric power to many areas.

The Great Migration from 1910-1970 re-shaped of both Southern states and Northern urban centers. In that period about 6 million African-Americans left the Southern states and moved to Northern cities where industrialization was growing at a rapid rate. Blacks moved to Chicago, Detroit, New York, Philadelphia, St Louis, and Washington, DC in numbers that had marked effects on employment, housing, schools, and politics in those areas.

When America entered the second World War African-American men were drafted into the military, but were kept in segregated groups. In the Territory of Hawaii Americans of Japanese ancestry volunteered for the army, and were assigned to a separate battalion that fought in Europe, after having their military training in segregated Southern states.

After FDR's death in 1945 and Harry Truman becoming President there was little indication that racial segregation would change, nor the alliance between 'old South' and Northern urban politicians would change the nature of the Democrat party. The open segregation and lynching of Black WW2 veterans in the South moved Truman to change his prior views favoring racial separation. He felt as President he should lead to reverse open racial segregation and hostility. In 1946 he formed the first national Commission on Civil Rights, with a call "To Secure These Rights." In 1947 he became the first U.S. President to speak at the convention of the National Association for Advancement of Colored People (NAACP.)

At the Democrat Convention of 1948, held in Philadelphia so new television networks could show it live on the East Coast, Senator Alban Barkley of Kentucky gave the keynote address pushing delegates to be optimistic for their chances to beat the Republican party in the coming election.

Minneapolis mayor Hubert Humphrey introduced a civil rights plank for the party's platform. It was adopted and many Southern delegates left the convention. Two weeks after the convention President Truman signed an Executive Order ending all racial discrimination in the US military.

Republicans nominated NY Gov. Tom Dewey, and a breakaway group of Southern "Dixiecrats" nominated Senator Strom Thurmond.

The 1948 election was a turning point in reshaping the direction and memberships of both the Democrat and Republican parties. Truman won the election, surprising many people.

CIVIL RIGHTS MOVEMENT EFFECT ON POLITICAL PARTIES

During the Eisenhower presidency,1953-1961, civil rights progress came largely from the courts and from citizens' actions. The 1954 Supreme Court decision, Brown vs Board of Education, made segregated schools unconstitutional. During Southern protests against desegregation, such as in Little Rock, Arkansas in 1957, Federal troops were used, by order of President Eisenhower, to protect Black students entering previously segregated schools.

As Congress failed to advance civil rights legislation it was citizen non-violent protests, such as the Birmingham, AL, bus boycott started by Rosa Parks, and other protests led by Rev. Martin Luther King, that increased national support for the movement. The 1960 election of Democrat John Kennedy over Republican Richard Nixon moved legislation for civil rights to the forefront of public awareness. After Kennedy's assassination in 1963 his successor, Lyndon Johnson, used his years of legislative experience to have Congress pass the Civil Rights Act of 1964 and the Voting Rights Act of 1965.

Though much progress was made in civil rights during the Johnson administration, continued civil unrest in 1968, mostly against the war in Vietnam but also for more progress in civil rights, brought the election of Republican Richard Nixon over Democrat Hubert Humphrey.

The Republican party campaign was led by advisors who had a definite Southern Strategy, by which Republican candidates appealed to white Southern racial grievances to reshape the political makeup of the region.

President Nixon showed an excellent view of geopolitics, as evidenced by his opening relations with communist China, and thereby starting a counter-balance to the Soviet Union's role in the Cold War that had persisted since 1946. Yet Nixon's political misdeeds caused his resignation and the presidency of Gerald Ford, 1974-1977. Popular antipathy against Nixon's Republican party and the Democrat's choice of a Southern Governor, Jimmy Carter, as candidate in the 1976 election, brought a pause in the Republican party's Southern Strategy.

Continued inflation and increasing unemployment, along with a hostage crisis in Iran, and an intra-party rivalry with Senator Ted Kennedy, doomed Carter's try for at a second term and brought the election of President Reagan in 1980. Reagan's communication skills as a former actor, and his framing the economic situation on too much government regulation, kept him popular for two terms. Reagan's Vice-President George H.W. Bush won the presidency in 1988, in an election marked by the Democrat party's personal and policy divisions.

In the 1992 presidential campaign civil rights protests, and other national economic issues led the Democrats to choose a Southern Governor, Bill Clinton, with veteran Senator Al Gore as his Vice-Presidential running mate. Clinton positioned himself as a 'New Democrat,' ready to cooperate with Republicans to work for a balanced budget, lower taxes for small businesses, and higher tax-rates on the very wealthy. Clinton brought middle-of-the-road social policies, and stronger anti-drug laws, thus co-opting Republican policies and easily winning re-election in 1996.

TWENTY FIRST CENTURY INTRA-PARTY CHANGES

The presidential election of 2000 was so closely contested that a Supreme Court ruling regarding counting of votes in Florida decided the outcome in favor of Republican George W. Bush. George W. Bush's re-election in 2004 was partly caused by support for him in time of the war in Iraq and partly by revival of the Southern Strategy begun by Nixon in 1972.

The 2008 election of Barack Obama as first African-American president was due to revitalization of 'get out the vote' campaigns by the Democrat party, and the result of community actions after years of civil rights protests. Obama's victory may have been partly due to the choice of Republican candidate McCain's Vice-Presidential running-mate Sarah Palin, who didn't meet the standards most Americans held for a person in that position. Obama won nearly 53% of the popular vote, to McCain's 45.7% Obama's campaign in 2012 against then former Massachusetts Governor Mitt Romney was focused on domestic economic issues and those related to the ongoing war in Iraq. Obama won that election, but by a narrower margin, 51.1% to Romney's 47.2%.

The 2016 Republican primary campaign, with 16 men and 1 woman competing for the nomination was hard-fought. Television personality Donald Trump won the nomination, despite public airing of some personal scandals. Trump chose Indiana Governor Mike Pence as his Vice-Presidential running-mate. The Democrats had several candidates formally declaring interest in running for the nomination, but only 5 had been elected to a political office. The Democrat convention nominated NY Senator and former Secretary of State Hillary Clinton, the first woman to receive presidential nomination from a major party.

H. Clinton (referred to thus to distinguish her from her husband former President Bill Clinton) chose VA Senator Tim Kaine as running-mate. H. Clinton's campaign focused on attacking Trump, and generally touting Democrat principles for labor, civil rights, and popular social-economic policies.

As sharp differences divided both Republicans and Democrats, two minor parties competed in the campaign. Libertarians nominated former NM Governor G. Johnson, and the Green Party nominated Jill Stein, both of whom drew off popular votes from both DEM and REP candidates in several states. Although Hillary Clinton received 2.87 million more popular votes than Trump, a total of only 80,000 votes for Trump in MI, PA and WI turned those states' 46 electoral votes to the Republican candidate. Though H. Clinton won 48.2% of the popular vote to Trump's 46.1%, the Republican candidate won 304 electoral votes to the Democrat's 227. Seven electors did not vote for any candidate.

DEMOGRAPHICS SHOW POLITICAL CHANGES

As a life-long history student I've found Demographics, discussed in the second essay of this collection, often reveal possible relations between events in different parts of a community, region, or nation. There is a concept termed 'concomitant variation,' that means in simple words, 'changes that <u>seem</u> to occur together.' The 'seem' is important as no cause-effect relationship is proven from the data alone. In the following discussion and charts I will try to show how changing demographics appear to have an effect on political outcomes. The United States' growth from 13 new states in an independent country to 50 states and territories from the Caribbean to the mid-Pacific Ocean came from many of the events discussed in this essay.

The 50 States, plus the District of Columbia, have disproportionate votes in determining the Executive and Legislative branches of our national government.

In the 50 states the population density goes from 1,260/ sq mi (NJ) and 1,059/sq mi (RI) down to 5.96/sq mi (WY) and 1.28/sq mi (AK.) Of ten states with the greatest population density (NJ, RI, MA, CT, MD, DE, NY, FL, PA, and OH in the 2020 presidential election all voted DEM except FL and OH. Of the ten states with the lowest population density (AK, WY, MT, SD, ND, NM, ID, NE & NV) in 2020 all voted REP except NM and NV. Other factors explain reasons those four states, FL, NM, NV, and OH, differ from others in this category. There are two other factors that I found significant in describing political differences among the 50 states.

There is a great variation among them as to what percent of their people have completed a four-year college education. Of the 20 states showing more than 35% of population having a four-year degree (CA, CO, CT, DE, HI, IL, KS, MA, MD, ME, MN, NH, NJ, NY, OR, RI, UT, VA, VT, and WA) only KS and UT voted REP in the 2020 election.

One other factor appears to have relationship with voting patterns. Our nation of immigrants has people from many different native countries. States vary significantly in the percentage of foreign-born citizens, first generation immigrants, who live in different states. More than 8.5% of citizens in 21 states were foreign born, (AZ, CA, CO, CT, DE, FL, GA, HI, IL, MA, MD, MN, NJ, NM, NV, NY, OR, RI, TX, VA, and WA.) All of those states voted DEM in 2020 except FL and TX. Only 6 of the other 29 states that had fewer than 8.5% foreign-born citizens (PA, MI, NH, WI, ME & VT) voted DEM in 2020 elections. These 3 New England states and 3 northern industrial states, each with fewer than 7.5% foreign-born citizens, voted DEM.

One analysis of the 2022 mid-term election shows the narrowest percentage differences in at least forty years between Democrat and Republican popular votes, for Senators in 36 states, for Governors in 36 states and for Congressional Representatives overall. As off-year, non-presidential elections have usually been won by the party not in the presidency, this 2022 election was surprisingly close by most measures. That article's author, a political data analyst for CNN, wrote 'neither party has a lasting majority from the public,' and believes the divisions in American society will continue in coming elections.

The author of this essay has a different opinion from that quoted above. I see implied results of demographic changes mean our nation may be at a time of changes of both Democrat and Republican parties, as in the time prior to the War Between the States.

I ask if our not-so-homogenous nation, in terms of urban vs rural communities; racial and ethnic differences; varying levels of education; can find a positive way to continue to function as one country, with a united set of values to present to an ever changing and interconnected world?

AFTERWORD

In these essays I have tried to report facts and trends as well as I have learned and can understand them, both in perspective of the times and social attitudes when they occurred, and with the implications for the diverse nation the United States has become today. I have tried to avoid showing a preference for one party over another.

Yet, as a serious life-long student of history I cannot avoid the view that the current Republican party, recently influenced by former President Trump's 'America First' nativism, and being heir to the Southern Strategy begun over 50 years ago under former President Nixon, is at great risk, as was the Whig party in the 1850s, of no longer being a viable political force in the coming decades.

Merle Fischlowitz
Honolulu, HI 2023

ABOUT THE AUTHOR

Author, In His Natural Habitat. 2013

Merle Fischlowitz, age 90 in 2022, is a native of St. Louis, MO. He earned a B.A. in History from Grinnell College, IA. His Ph.D. is from St. Louis University, a Jesuit school. Merle identifies as a "Jewish man with a Jesuit education, or the best of all possible worlds."

He has worked in school psychological services in Missouri, and Washington, DC, and psychologist in private practice in Honolulu, HI.

A life-long student of history, Merle has also published <u>From Dirt Paths to Golden Streets, Poems of Immigrant Experiences,</u> and <u>From Barbed Wire to Picket Fence; A Child Holocaust Survivor's Story,</u> about his late former wife Teresa Fischlowitz.

His other published books include <u>Oh, The Changes I Have Seen: Second Edition,</u> a personal memoir of changes in technologies he has known in his life-time.

Printed in the United States
by Baker & Taylor Publisher Services